Financial Wellness Featuring Edge 401(k) Funds

How to Improve the Retirement Outcomes of Your Employees

Thomas Ruggie, ChFC®, CFP® &
Michael Case Smith

Financial Wellness Featuring Edge 401(k) Funds

Published by:
90-Minute Books
Newinformation Inc
302 Martinique Drive
Winter Haven, FL 33884
www.90minutebooks.com

Copyright © 2015, Thomas Ruggie, ChFC®, CFP® & Michael Case Smith

Published in the United States of America

ISBN-13: 978-0692449011
ISBN-10: 0692449019

For more information on 90-Minute Books including finding out how you can publish your own lead generating book, visit www.90minutebook.com or call (863) 318-0464

Here's What's Inside…

Introduction

Here's the dirty little secret about 401 (k): Wall Street will not give true service to your employees until they are ready to roll over their $100,000⁺ balances to high-fee Individual Retirement Accounts(IRA).

Their legion of brokers will sell you a 401(k) then turn over the service of employees to the vendor's toll-free number and website, leaving those brokers free to cross-sell to high-net-worth employees. The last thing Wall Street brokers want to do is talk to new- hires about their budgets or credit card debt. But since these and other causes of financial stress directly impact your bottom line, a void exists in the market.

Edge 401(k) Funds, specifically the RWM Asset Management Collective Trust, solve the "who pays?" problem of financial wellness by building the expense of the money coaching service into the Fund fees.

We solve the "engaging the uninvolved" employee problem by turning the business model of medical and financial wellness upside down. We don't put up posters in break rooms and wait for calls. Rather, our coaches proactively make outbound calls to Fund participants …three times a year.

About RWM Asset Management Collective Trusts

Referred herein as, "Funds" or the "Edge 401(k) Funds", they include the Edge Conservative, Edge Moderate, and Edge Growth Funds. The subadvisor to the Funds is RWM Asset Management ("RWM"). RWM is a SEC-registered investment advisor headed by professionals who have worked with more than 700 retirement plans nationwide. A copy of the firm's current disclosure statement is available upon request. For more information, please visit http://edge401kfunds.com.

About Alta Trust Company

Alta Trust Company is a South Dakota chartered trust company that partners with investment managers such as RWM to offer unique collective investment fund solutions to the retirement plan marketplace. Alta Trust is not associated with the additional wellness benefits offered through RWM Asset Management Collective Trusts.

Chapter I

401(k) plans: the bedrock of retirement savings

In the early 1980s, 401(k) plans were only available at a handful of large companies.

Today, some 90 million Americans are covered by 640,000 401(k) plans.[i]

If your 401(k) plan is like most, it was sold by a stock or life insurance broker, is administered by a big fund or insurance complex, has lots of mutual funds and annuities, and provides nominal employee education. One 401(k) plan looks very much like every other.

In 2008, the financial crisis put the focus on fees and the regulatory reaction aimed at creating more transparency.

Despite the evolution of plan design, fee structures, and regulatory changes, what has not shown meaningful improvement is the result achieved by participants. And their retirement security is why 401(k) was developed.

Here is what we think is wrong with typical 401(k) plans:

1. The fees are still too high

According to the US General Accounting Office, each 1% of vendor fees reduces money at retirement by almost 20%.[ii] If your ATM kept $4 every time you took out a $20, you would notice, right?

Fee Impact on 401(k) Balances at Retirement

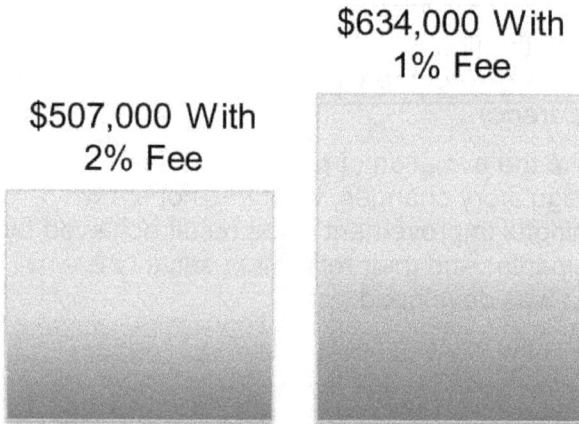

$634,000 With
1% Fee

$507,000 With
2% Fee

Scenario: $30k salary at age 30 with 3% merit raise per year to age 65.
$30k beginning 401(k) balance with deferral/match of 7%/year; self-
selected funds annual return 6.9% (Source: AON/Financial Engines May
2014 "Help in Defined Contribution Plans: 2006 through 2012"); Source
of fee impact is GAO. Source of balance at retirement is Bankrate.com
scenario modeling tools with the above scenario.

2. Employee do-it-yourself investing doesn't work

Numerous studies confirm what we've known for years: do-it-yourself investors do not perform as well as they could:

One recent study by Dalbar Inc., found that a typical investor in US stock mutual funds earned 3.7% per year over the past two decades, while the market generated returns of 11.1%.

Another study showed that those who either follow the investment allocation advice of a professional, or give portfolio management discretion to professionals through balanced, target date, or target risk funds increase their annual returns from 6.09% to 10.3%. [iii]

Professional Management Impact on 401(k) Balances at Retirement

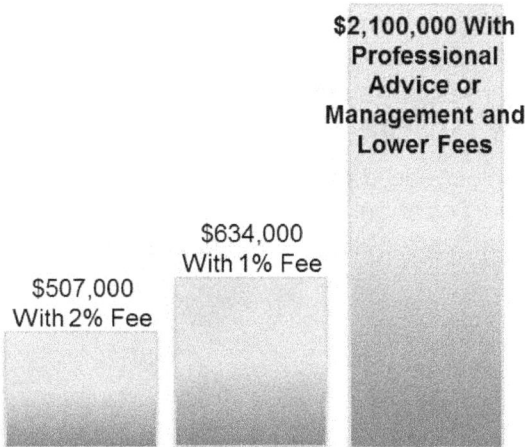

$2,100,000 With
Professional
Advice or
Management and
Lower Fees

$634,000
With 1% Fee

$507,000
With 2% Fee

See chart above for scenario sources, inputs, and modeling tools.

3. Traditional employee education doesn't work

401(k) websites, brochures, and education meetings have been shown to have little effect on financial behavior. That is because, based on our experience, employees fall into two groups, both ill-served by traditional 401(k)s:

(a) Sophisticated Investors

Often highly compensated, you will probably never see them at enrollment meetings. They work with their own stock broker or want access to more than the 20-30 mutual funds on a traditional 401(k) roster so they may self-manage their portfolios.

(b) Everyone Else

We call these investors 'uninvolved.' Their needs are typically much different than sophisticated or involved investors. Many stress about money and are confused over how to invest, where to invest, and how much to invest. Many do not have anyone to turn to for assistance, and qualified financial planners are not beating their doors down to proactively assist them.

We have discovered that there is a tremendous amount of frustration, and it's not getting any better as Americans struggle to achieve financial wellness and save for retirement.

Chapter II

It started with a drive

In 2013, Insurance Office of America (IOA), one of the nation's largest independent commercial risk and benefit managers, turned to us to develop a better retirement programs for their 30,000 clients.[iv]

Tom, an Investment Advisor and veteran consultant to over 700 plans, knew that traditional 401(k) education is ineffective for most employees who are dealing with a myriad of financial issues outside their 401(k) plans.

Michael, having testified at United States Senate, Securities and Exchange Commission, and Department of Labor hearings on Wall Street conflicts of interest, knew that traditional 401(k) funds were not the answer, either.[v]

So, one day, as we were driving to a 401(k) enrollment meeting, we started discussing what it would take to engage employees in more meaningful ways. At that meeting, we began asking questions about their financial stress levels and listened carefully to the answers. We heard things the firm's HR executive Connie (and HR executives nationwide) have known for some time:

Traditional 401(k) plans, with their nicely-produced brochures and videos, didn't go far enough to 'move the dial' toward engaging participants, helping them reach their retirement goals.

Further, the industry offers little or nothing to coach them on the things that could make them financially healthier employees for the 'Connies' of the world: such as how to make prudent decisions about budget, debt, and planning for life's little surprises.

Together, we formed the vision for a financial wellness service inside a 401(k) fund which would proactively offer education on 401(k), sure, but also a personal advisor who would provide information on other financial areas such as budgeting, debt management, funding education, and overall savings.

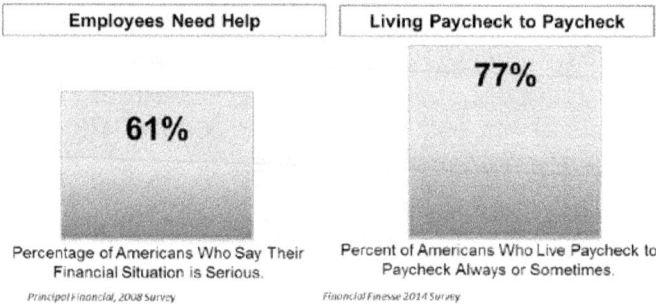

Employees Need Help	Living Paycheck to Paycheck
61%	**77%**

Percentage of Americans Who Say Their Financial Situation is Serious.

Principal Financial, 2008 Survey

Percent of Americans Who Live Paycheck to Paycheck Always or Sometimes.

Financial Finesse 2014 Survey

The problem to be solved

Corporate profit goes up when medical claims go down. Simple.

As noted in the Wall Street Journal, "Nearly 90% of employers offer wellness incentives"[vi]. A primary reason seems to be to control medical costs, which often result from employees' poor lifestyle choices.

Taking that a step further, more than 200 studies have shown that financial stress is a key cause of those poor lifestyle choices. Unhealthy financial stress relievers like burgers, beers, and brownies drive many of the downstream medical claims those 90% of employers are trying, and paying, to reduce.

So, it seemed clear to us that if companies could offer financial wellness programs that complement their health campaigns, results of both the 401(k) and medical wellness programs would improve.

In researching the market, however, we found that,

There are financial wellness Employee Assistance Programs (EAPs) that provide seminars, research, and take inbound calls for a hard-dollar cost of $50-150/head - a hard dollar cost few employers seem willing to absorb.

There are Wall Street firms who re-package investment advice as financial wellness, but they do not effectively address other areas of life – including some of the real drivers of financial stress.

And there are business-to-consumer tools that offer planning and counseling. However, this requires the uninvolved participant to take two unlikely steps: 1) Opt into the financial wellness product, and 2) actually pay the hard-dollar costs associated with these products, typically $25-$40 per month.

Historically, the problem was that neither Wall Street nor medical wellness providers have reached out to employees to do the hard work of counseling them on their finances, one-on-one. So we needed to overcome two critical hurdles: who pays and how to engage uninvolved employees.

The Solution

So, to fill the void in the market for effective (…and cost effective) financial wellness counseling, we helped develop a program that makes a money coach available "inside" a 401(k) fund.

OK, first the legal stuff. The offering is called RWM Asset Management Collective Trust. Alta Trust Company, a chartered trust company is the manager and the asset allocation is subadvised by RWM Asset Management (RWM), Tom's investment management firm – see the endnote and bio for his credentials and recognitions.[vii] The Fund Series is known as the Edge Conservative, Edge Moderate, and Edge Growth Funds (or for our purposes here, the "Funds" or the Edge 401(k) Funds). The financial wellness component we describe is managed by RWM and is separate and independent from Alta Trust. So Alta Trust makes it tradable on a 401(k) platform and RWM adds (1) asset allocation within the Funds and (2) access to a money coach independent of Alta. And while we are at it with legal, none of these entities are affiliated with Insurance Office of America or Asset Advisors of America.

Now, back to the story!

These Edge 401(k) Funds, again the RWM Asset Management Collective Trust, solve the "who pays?" problem by building the expense of the coaching service into the Fund fee, also called fund operating expenses. Think of the financial wellness component as an 'aftermarket' addition to the Edge 401(k) Funds.

We solve the "engaging the uninvolved" problem by turning the business model of the EAPs upside down. We don't put up a poster in the break room and wait for calls. Rather, our coaches make outbound calls to participants invested in the Funds three times a year.

The launch of the Funds was covered nationwide by media outlets, many of whom followed up with interviews and articles about this exciting new direction in financial wellness. Some realized right away why this financial wellness coaching component could improve the well-being of employees and companies – and was the logical next step as a complement to medical wellness.

As more and more businesses recognize the proven importance of financial wellness initiatives as part of a healthy workforce and overall employee productivity, we believe our innovative approach will help solve concerns and reduce hard costs related to financial-related stress.

Bottom line: our financial wellness coaching comes at no hard-dollar cost. Therefore, improvements in turnover, medical claims, and other downstream benefits realized go straight to the bottom line of the company sponsoring the 401(k).

Chapter III

Lowered financial stress, increased productivity: how financial wellness can benefit employers/plan sponsors.

The financial wellness component from RWM money coaches help employers prioritize retirement readiness.

As the money coaches work with participants invested in the Funds on their short-range financial goals, they may help ease financial stress, which can increase productivity and employee satisfaction.

According to over 200 academic studies, when employees improve their financial well-being, many see their health improve; they are more productive and more likely to stay with the company. This creates an opportunity for happier employees and a more profitable company. With the addition of a full-service financial wellness program, employers may see:

Productivity and performance improve

Financial liabilities mitigated

Absenteeism decrease

Turnover decrease

Healthcare costs decrease

Pay satisfaction increase

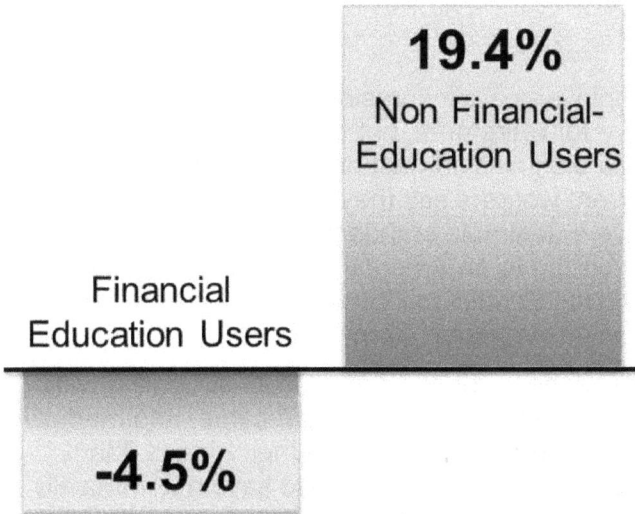

Change in One Company's Healthcare Costs from 2010 to 2012

19.4%
Non Financial-Education Users

Financial Education Users

-4.5%

Source: Financial Finesse Reports

Chapter IV

Gaining a stronger financial footing and relieving financial stress: how financial wellness can benefit employees.

Employees are increasingly making an effort to save for retirement, but are still finding it difficult to build a significant nest egg. Less than half of current workers say they are saving enough to have a desirable standard of living in retirement, according to an *America Saves and American Savings Education Council* survey conducted by Opinion Research Corp.

The reasons run the gamut from struggling with debt from school loans, credit cards, and medical bills to simply living beyond their means. Many people have never learned to save automatically outside of a workplace retirement account. Others don't consider it a priority, while many more would like to save but simply can't because their income barely covers their expenses. Since the bursting of the housing bubble, many people still have a home that is worth less than the balance of the outstanding mortgage.

According to Dallas Salisbury, President of the Employee Benefit Research Institute, about half of Americans say they sometimes receive financial windfalls, including tax refunds, gifts, bonuses, or inheritances. Most who receive a cash windfall (39%) save at least part of it, but according to US News and World Report, "*7 Reasons Americans Can't Save for Retirement*" on Feb. 23, 2011, 10% generally spend it all.

According to The American Psychological Association (APA), financial stress is the leading cause of unhealthy behaviors like smoking, weight gain, and alcohol and drug abuse.

A 2012 Financial Education 'Initiatives in the Workplace' study reported that 85% of HR professionals indicated that personal financial challenges had a large impact on overall employee performance, and a survey by the Kaiser Family Foundation indicated that 61% of Americans say they perceive their financial situation is serious.

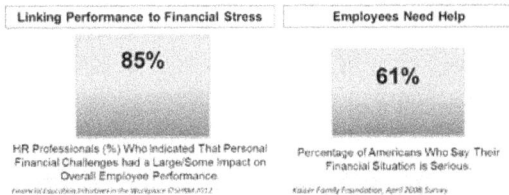

Linking Performance to Financial Stress	Employees Need Help
85%	61%
HR Professionals (%) Who Indicated That Personal Financial Challenges had a Large/Some Impact on Overall Employee Performance.	Percentage of Americans Who Say Their Financial Situation is Serious.
Financial Education Initiatives in the Workplace (SHRM) 2012	Kaiser Family Foundation, April 2008 Survey

In the U.S., 69% of parents surveyed can't save for their children's higher education because everyday living expenses have left no additional funds.

While saving for retirement is often touted as the most important financial objective, it is far from the only financial concern many individuals struggle with. They often need help with other financial concerns such as budgeting, debt elimination, investment principles, tax strategies, and estate planning.

Chapter V

What is financial wellness coaching? How does it work?

"The dominant determinant of lifetime investment outcomes is not investment performance but investor behavior."

In developing our model, we looked at who would potentially benefit from this type of service. First of all, you have about 15% of employees who are 'involved participants,' the do-it-yourselfers who don't need the help of a financial advisor or who have a financial advisor already in place.

Our audience is primarily the other 85%, the uninvolved. These are participants who know they can't do it themselves and know they need the help, but typically don't have the means or the confidence to go out and get the necessary support they need. Our goal is to provide them with that financial planning help.

Some plans choose to simply add the Funds to their existing roster, and that's fine.

Some close down existing professionally-managed funds, such as target date or risk-based funds and transfer balances to the Funds, and that's fine too.

After documenting a prudent selection process, typically a phone call and signature on a fund addition form is all it takes to add Edge 401(k) Funds to an existing investment roster. From there, we schedule a launch meeting or webinar introducing the new financial wellness benefit to staff. A video is prepared for those who are offsite and for future hires explaining the offer.

Participants who have money ...any money, meaning even a small allocation, to these Funds are proactively contacted by qualified customer relationship managers three times a year.

These relationship managers first schedule time for participants to speak with a financial wellness coach who will onboard them and walk them through what they need to know about their 401(k) plans, using questionnaires to help them determine their risk pattern, how much they should be investing, and where they should be properly investing, be it Edge 401(k) or other roster funds. These talks will also open the door to discussing other pertinent financial needs such as budgeting, debt management/consolidation, funding education, and overall savings plans.

Financial wellness coaches will also offer to walk participants through a retirement planning process to determine if they're on track with their retirement goals while addressing other related topics, such as whether needed insurance and legal documents are in place. We can be as comprehensive as each client needs.

In a traditional broker-sold 401(k), annual plan reviews discuss investment performance and perhaps highlight how many times an employee called-in to a vendor's toll-free number, which is typically 5-10% from our experience.

In contrast, we are able to show specific before and after improvements to those who work with a financial wellness counselor on savings and projected income at retirement.

Participants are encouraged to reach out via email or a toll-free number to their financial wellness coaches any time they have financial questions.

If we don't hear from them, no problem, they will still receive outbound calls or texts to let them know what's going on with their investment in Edge 401(k) Funds, again the RWM Asset Management Collective Trust, three times a year.

At some point, employees will have life events or decide to take steps to address financial stressors.

From our experience, HR executives are very happy they have a resource.

Our coaching is backed by the knowledge and expertise of Investment Advisors and experienced Certified Financial Planners™ who provide employees with the tools they need to make informed financial decisions, and to help empower them to be more comfortable about how they manage their money.

Our confidential approach takes into account employee needs and learning styles. By assessing employees' financial vulnerabilities and strengths, we help them customize personal financial plans of action.

We know that having such a plan is only half the battle; moving consistently toward their desired financial goals is the other key to success. We put together an action plan, including deadlines and what the follow-up process is going to be. This accountability helps reduce procrastination and life distractions that often get in the way.

We believe this formula for success works at a deep level to produce change.

Each financial wellness coaching session provides a confidential, non-judgmental forum with an expert dedicated to that employee. While receiving help with financial goals, employees may find this assistance positively impacts their whole life. The result is often increased self-awareness and increased happiness.

Case Studies: When life happens, having a trusted financial coach you can turn to can reduce stress.

When a client's father passed away, she was left with a large inheritance and little idea of what to do with it. Our advisor was able to talk her step-by-step through the options, and even joined in a conference call with the client and her estate attorney as they discussed drawing up trust documents. Today, this client considers her advisor a trusted friend.

Dealing with the anguish of his wife's cancer and then with her loss, left one client over his head emotionally--and drained financially. Our advisor talked with him and recognized he could get the money he needed to live on by refinancing his home. Since the original loan was in both the husband and wife's names, our advisor was able to connect him with a mortgage broker who was able to get the home refinanced in his name only, and actually reduced his mortgage rate. This involvement kept him from withdrawing everything out of his retirement account.

A stay-at-home mom for 35 years found herself going through a divorce. Stressful enough on its surface, it was further complicated by the fact that she had not earned income in her name. Building credit and getting her home placed in her name were facilitated by our advisor who helped the woman create and implement a workable financial plan for her future.

Chapter VI

How are the Funds managed?

The Funds are managed by RWM Asset Management with the guideline of the Morningstar® Indexes. We use the Morningstar Conservative, Morningstar Moderate Portfolio, and the Morningstar Aggressive Growth, so, effectively, we're benchmarking against those three funds.

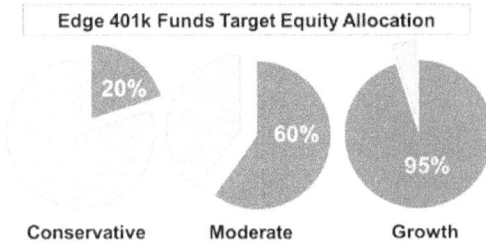

Edge 401k Funds Target Equity Allocation

| Conservative | Moderate | Growth |
| 20% | 60% | 95% |

Morningstar Indexes combine the science and art of indexing to give investors a clearer view into the world's financial markets. They also serve as a precise benchmarking resource.

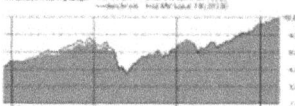

We maintain a similar allocation to the benchmarks. Tactical adjustments are made against the index with a goal of outperforming the index, but we do not deviate much plus or minus from how the indexes are performing.

We're structured so we're investing similarly to the index and making strategic or tactical adjustments within the portfolio based on what's going on in the current economy and investment world.

The rationale behind this

The reality is, numerous studies have shown that when it comes to 401(k) plans, individuals investing on their own do much worse than those investing with a financial advisor. The more we looked into this for our model, we realized investment returns are important, but what's most important for the 85% we are targeting is behavioral patterns.

When left on their own, participants tend to buy at the wrong time (when everything is going gangbusters) and sell at the wrong time (when things are doing very poorly) without looking at the big picture and long-term growth. Uncontrolled behavior patterns lead to bad decisions.

Chapter VII

Do we need to change our entire plan?

Like your current 401(k) advisor? That's fine. We want to complement, not compete, with quality brokers.

In fact, we have relationships with many financial advisors across the country. We focus on our specialties: plan consulting and financial wellness, so they can focus on business owners and key executives.

Don't want to hassle moving your plan? No problem, Edge 401(k) Funds are available on over 20 major 401(k) platforms, and many large insurance companies, so they can be added to an existing plan or included as part of a new 401(k) plan.

Vendors with whom Alta Trust, Funds trustee, has agreements include:

Ascensus

BMO

BPAS

Charles Schwab

Fidelity

Great West/Empower

John Hancock

Mass Mutual

MG Trust (Matrix)

Mid Atlantic Trust

One America

Paychex

Principal Financial Group

Reliance Trust

TD Ameritrade Trust

Transamerica

Vanguard

Why has this not been available before?

We feel this has not been available before because no other company or fund was willing to make this type of an investment in the future of participants just because it was the right thing to do. We feel like by building a better model, as our clients succeed, we will, too.

Chapter XIII

Aside from financial wellness, what else should we expect from our plan?

While we often work with existing brokers, members of our staff and related firms are fiduciary advisors to plan sponsors. In this role, we put ourselves in your shoes to make certain everything is structured the way it should be, with a focus on your best interests.

From the financial wellness standpoint, the benefits are significant for the company and participants. The expectation should be for a tremendous value-added service benefiting both parties.

From the plan stewardship standpoint, our consultants act as your in-house specialists to help your efforts to keep the plan in compliance and protect you from liabilities.

To help you, we've developed a simple ten-question fiduciary scoring system.

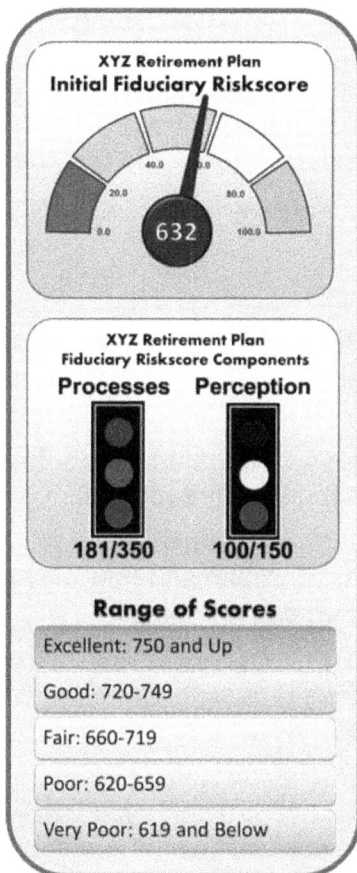

XYZ Retirement Plan
Initial Fiduciary Riskscore

632

40.0   60.0
20.0   80.0
0.0   100.0

XYZ Retirement Plan
Fiduciary Riskscore Components

Processes   **Perception**

181/350   100/150

Range of Scores

Excellent: 750 and Up

Good: 720-749

Fair: 660-719

Poor: 620-659

Very Poor: 619 and Below

As retirement savings programs are increasingly a focus for regulators and class-action lawyers, we developed this simple survey to help identify fiduciary weaknesses in order to then implement improvements.

At the end of the process, we fill the gap between current and best practices.

Here's why that's important: The Department of Labor has hired an army of investigators whose job is to generate penalty income from businesses like yours. In Florida alone, there are 70 investigators conducting audits. Three years ago there were two.

Our clients can answer their questions in these areas:

PLAN DESIGN - How did you decide on the current plan design and how often do you review it against market competitors?

FEES – Have you evaluated vendor fees to ensure they are necessary and reasonable?

INVESTMENTS - Can you document how the funds were added to your plan and how they are monitored on an ongoing basis?

STEWARDSHIP – Can you produce key plan documents upon request? Have plan fiduciaries been identified and understand their roles under ERISA?

EDUCATION - Are you confident that your employees have been given the resources to understand the plan and reach their retirement goals?

In Conclusion

Investment advice has become a commodity. From "robo-advisors" to target-date funds, the role of the traditional broker is being marginalized.

Further, as we go to print, the United States Department of Labor has proposed rules that will force the brokerage industry to put the financial interests of their clients before theirs. Called the "Fiduciary Standard" many feel it will begin a seminal change in the value proposition of brokers.

In light of these developments, we envision a world where those who work with 90 million Americans covered by 640,000 401(k) plans add value by delivering financial wellness, not stock and fund picks.

We welcome your thoughts and are available to meet with your 401(k) committee to better understand the new world of 401(k).

Thomas H. Ruggie, ChFC®, CFP®

President

- 24 years in the financial industry
- Barron's Top 1200 Advisors[1]; 50 Fastest Growing RIA Firms[2];
- Top 100 Wealth Managers[3]; Top RIA's/List of Fastest-Growing Firms[4];
- Top 100 Independent Advisors[5]; Top 100, Top 40 Most Influential Advisors[6];
- Top Wealth Managers[7]; Top Wealth Advisors[8]

Michael Case Smith

Managing Director

- Testified on Wall Street conflicts for the SEC, DoL, and US Senate
- Strategist for JP Morgan, AIG, NY Life
- Target Date Fund Portfolio Manager at Avatar Associates
- Target Date Fund Index Manager of the TD Ameritrade's Independence ETFs
- UCLA, Notre Dame, London School of Economics

[1] *Barron's February 2015, February 2013, February 2009;* [2] *Financial Advisor Magazine 2011;* [3] *Advisor One 2011* [4] *Financial Advisor Magazine 2013, 2011, 2010;* [5] *Registered Rep Magazine 2011, 2010;* [6] *401k Wire 2011, 2010;* [7] *Wealth Manager Web 2011, 2010;* [8] *Worth Magazine 2006, 2007, 2008*

[i] DOL Employee Benefits Security Administration, Private Pension
Plan Bulletin:
Abstract of 2011 Form 5500 Annual Reports
, June
2013

[ii] "Changes Needed to Provide 401(k) Plan Participants and the Department of Labor Better Information on Fees" United States Government Accountability Office; November 2006

[iii] Quantitative Analysis of Investor Behavior 2014", Dalbar Inc. and AON/Financial Engines May 2014 "Help in Defined Contribution Plans: 2006 through 2012"

[iv] Edge (a dba of RWM Asset Management), Alta Trust, and Insurance Office of America are not affiliated companies.

[v] US Senate Special Committee on Aging 10/2009; SEC/DOL Joint Hearing on Target Date Funds 6/2009

[vi] "Your Company Wants to Make You Healthy" Wall St. Journal April 8, 2013 Article notes, "That's up from 57% of companies in 2009."

[vii] *Barron's Top 1000 Advisors* Barron's February 2013, February 2009, *50 Fastest Growing RIA Firms* Financial Advisor Magazine 2011, *Top 100 Wealth Managers* Advisor One 2011, *Top RIA's/List of Fastest-Growing Firms* Financial Advisor Magazine 2013, 2011, 2010, *Top 100 Independent Advisors* Financial Advisor Magazine 2013, 2011, 2010, *Top 100, Top 40 Most Influential Advisor* Registered Rep Magazine 2011, 2010, *Top Wealth Managers* Wealth Manager Web 2011, 2010, *Top Wealth Advisors* Worth Magazine 2006, 2007, 2008

www.ingramcontent.com/pod-product-compliance
Lightning Source LLC
Chambersburg PA
CBHW060501210326
41520CB00015B/4054